Darling, I want you to know how very special you are to me

By Bernard Levine

'I'm so grateful for your love
and here is your reminder why I love
you.'

Surprise your loved one today with
an exciting
romantic message.

Inside this unique book, you will find
a collection of
exciting romantic words to express
your feelings and your affection to
your loved one.

Baby

I love being with you.

You inspire me to achieve

my ambitions

You fill my world with surprises

I feel I have found a new life.

In my mind you are adorable

In my heart you are completeness

I am yours totally

In support

Through all our tomorrows.

What is this thing called love?

Daisy and Tuck were Mom and
Dad's friends.
We would often go and visit them

on the weekend.

They were customers and supported all the suburban businesses by having accounts at the butchery, the hardware store, the petrol station, the pharmacy, the corner cafe and even our local cinema.

Daisy loved buying the most expensive bottles of perfume that she could find…while Tuck felt that he just didn't have enough fishing tackle, tools and hardware and would carry on buying more and more.

At the end of the month, when they received their account statements, there was never enough money to pay for everything.

So, what they would do was pay $50 to the one business and $100 to another store.

Often, while visiting Daisy and Tuck at their home, it was the norm to see them argue about their money situation.

One Sunday afternoon, Daisy got behind the couch where Tuck was sitting and then went and hit Tuck on the head with her frying pan...as she ran away, Tuck would grab objects like the glass vase and throw it straight at Daisy.

This carried on and on and Daisy would duck and throw her

porcelain plates at Tuck, bending low to avoid being hit by the flying objects that Tuck was throwing at her.
Eventually, they both stopped, tired and exhausted sitting down and talking to each other as if nothing had happened at all.
Daisy and Tuck have been happily married for more than 40 years, and the one partner couldn't live without the other.
So, what's the moral of the story? No matter what happens, come what may, true love will never die...through thick and thin, they stick together for better or worse.

The Glory of Love

You've got to give a little, take a little,
and let your poor heart break a little.
That's the story of, that's the glory of love.
You've got to laugh a little, cry a little,
until the clouds roll by a little.
That's the story of, that's the glory of love.
You've got to win a little, lose a little,
yes, and always have the blues a little.
That's the story of, that's the glory of love.

Music and lyrics by Billy Hill

If I could be ...

The sun shining down on your face

The soft breeze blowing through your hair

If I could be ...

The ring you wear on your hand

The food you taste and bite

The spot where you sit or stand

The blanket that covers you at night.

If I could only be ...

Lessons in love

I was invited to have lunch with Rev Charlie and Sylvia.
When I arrived at their home, I felt that there was something that just didn't feel right.
Rev Charlie took me aside...
'My wife and I had a terrible argument this
morning and now she's not talking to me...
I was going to cancel our lunch arrangement, but I couldn't get hold of you...

...but never mind, I'm glad that you are now
here...
I have a brilliant idea of how I'm going to make it up and apologise to Sylvia....
Come look and see what I have done...
Rev Charlie took me to the bathroom.
I was very surprised to see that floating in the
bath-water were lots of red carnation flower petals.
'Come with me, let's go have a drink at the pool...
What would you like to have?'
While we were basking in the

sun, it wasn't long afterwards
that Sylvia came outside making
her way straight to Rev Charlie.
Sylvia bent down and gave Rev
Charlie a big hug, with tears in
her eyes.
Rev Charlie's idea had worked
and love had won the day!

Remember

**That surprise phone-call just
to say "Hello"**

**The passionate kiss that
almost left us breathless**

**The sweet love-note which
said 'Thank You!'**

When we couldn't say "Bye-Bye."

Remember

My darling wherever you go

I adore you, as each moment grows

So much more than I've ever done before

Remember, Remember

I need you now and for evermore!

Imagine the look on your loved one's face

to discover a secret love-note
hidden in the fridge or the
surprise of finding an apple
with a ribbon tied all-around
placed under the pillow.
For a very exciting reaction, leave flower
petals floating in the bathwater.
Do something special for your
loved one today trying different
pleasant 'surprises'
and the flame of love will burn
forever brightly.

Secrets of Love

Make your love one feel special
every day.

Do not allow your lives to become routine -
prepare lots of different activities to enjoy.
Never take your loved one for granted.
Keep your love forever precious, sacred and beautiful.
What you put into your love
is what you will get out of your love.
Enrich your lives with prayer.
Always be your partner's best friend.

A VERY BEAUTIFUL LOVE

You touch my heart with precious love songs

You cover my body with poetry

You make me feel that you really care.

A thousand kisses

A million dreams

You are heaven to me.

I will always love you

Now and forever

So very, very deeply.

How far would you go to please the one you love?

Love makes us do the strangest things.

My Dad owned a Toy Shop called Continental Novelties and specialized in selling jokes and tricks like itchy powder, stink bombs and poo-poo cushions. A regular customer who loved coming to talk to my Dad, was Jock Simmonds.

'You see this finger' Jock showed my Dad his middle finger of his left hand.

'Tomorrow, I'm going to cut it right off!'

Jock explained that his wife, Emma wanted him to buy her a hi-fi set which he couldn't afford....so, he had an idea of how he would be able to get the money to please Emma to buy her the hi-fi set.

'What I'm going to do', Jock explained 'you see, at the factory where I work there is an electric saw that I work with...

so, what I'm going to do is close my eyes and stick my middle finger in front of the electric saw and Voopa! It will be off! Then I will get $1000 from the Workman's Compensation at my work and I'll be able to get my

wife the hi-fi that she wants.'
My Dad told Jock that he was
mad!
Three weeks later, Jock came to
visit my Dad at the shop minus his
left hand middle finger.
'You see this thumb', Jock
showed my Dad his right hand
thumb...
'if I pretend that it's an accident
and put my right thumb in front
of the electric saw, I will get paid
$2500.
I really love my wife so much and
she so dearly wants me to buy
her a dish-washer but I just don't
have the cash. I don't have the
heart to not give her what she

wants, so I'm going to do it!'

My Dad didn't see Jock for several months, when suddenly one day, Jock arrived at the shop with 3 of his fingers missing...his right hand thumb was gone as well as his left hand middle finger and what really surprised

my Dad the most, was to see that his left hand pinkie was also cut off.

Jock was very sad...

'you know what happened Mr Levine, you see my bosses at work became suspicious as this was now the third time that I had put in an accident claim when I cut off my pinkie ...they couldn't

understand why it was always just happening to me and guess what?...the Workman's Compensation refused to pay out my claim! Then, to make matters worse, because I didn't get the money, I couldn't buy my wife the ruby ring that she wanted...so she left me for another man!'
What's the moral of this story? Money can't really buy you love.

For You, My Darling

There's nothing more precious

than your love
There's nothing more beautiful
than your smile
There's nothing more inspiring
than your kiss
No one can thrill me like you do
You are my dream come true!

'The greatest thing
You'll ever learn
Is just to love and be loved in
return'

Lyrics from Nature Boy by Eden Ahbez.

Love grows when you let someone know that you care.

A Lifetime of Love

Darling,

In my eyes I see you as the most

beautiful marvel of creation

In my arms your very presence is

heavenly inspiration

From the heart to the heart

I mean every word I say

With my body to your body

I will adore you in every way

With my life I surrender

my entire being beyond
compare

Through all my days

And in all my nights

To cherish

To care

To always be

Forever yours

Getting to know you

My friend Johnny was given a
girl's contact phone number.
'Hi Lucy, my name is Johnny...
I was given your phone number
by a mutual friend of ours,
Gordon Green...
I would like to meet you.
Would you like to go to movie?'
Lucy replied: 'No! I'm not a
prostitute...
I won't go out with you to a
movie'.
Johnny was very surprised by
Lucy's answer.
'Alright, Lucy...then shall we go
out for
dinner?

I know a very nice restaurant I think you'll love'.
Lucy's remark was firm:
'I'm not a hoar...you can't buy me!'
Johnny was puzzled and didn't know what to do.
'Lucy, would you prefer going out for coffee?'
'Johnny, how many times must I tell you that I'm not a prostitute'.
Johnny was about to give up and put the phone down, but he thought he'll try just one more time...
'Tell me Lucy...I really want to meet you...how do you suggest we meet?'

What Lucy said next shocked
Johnny.
'Please take me to the fields!
What are you doing this coming
Sunday morning?
Could you come to my home at 6
in the
morning?'
Johnny's mind began to wander...
He could not believe what he had
just heard.
Sunday morning came around
and Johnny was up bright and
early...he could hardly wait to
meet his date.
Lucy and Johnny drove away in
Johnny's car and when Johnny
turned the corner, Lucy pointed

out the field.
'Johnny, please stop! This is where I want you to take me.'
As they walked through the tall grass, Lucy found an Aloe succulent plant.
'Johnny, are you thirsty? Let's have something to drink!'
Johnny blurted out:
'I don't see any stream or water here...we're in the middle of the field...there's absolutely not a drop to drink here!'
Lucy tugged hard on the Aloe succulent plant:
'Johnny, help me pull this plant out of the
ground'.

Lucy then took the plant and hit it hard against a rock to break and get the plant to open.
'Here Johnny, suck!'
Johnny was scared.
'No Lucy, you go first!'
Lucy showed Johnny the way to do it...and once Johnny had seen Lucy enjoying the juices of the Aloe plant, he also partook and loved the refreshing taste.
'Johnny, have you eaten breakfast?
There is so much food here to eat...I don't know where to begin...
Look there's wild plum and wild fig...

And over there we have the Num-
Num tree with very tasty
fruit...what do you feel like?'
This date was surely a most
interesting experience that
Johnny will always remember.
They then drove back to Lucy's
home.
When they arrived at Lucy's
apartment, Johnny couldn't help
but ask:
'Lucy, it smells so good
here...what is the name of the
fragrance or perfume that you
have been spraying in the room?'
Lucy took Johnny by the hand...
'Come let me show you!'
Behind the couch, Lucy showed

Johnny a small piece of pantyhose which she had cut and filled with some rose petals…
'It's called potpourri', she told Johnny.
'What kind of music do you like Lucy?'
'Johnny, I find music so very boring…it's always the same lyrics repeated over and over again and the tunes are all so monotonous. The music that I really like are film sound-tracks because you can listen to it hundreds of times and every time you will hear something different like an instrument that you have never heard before'.

'Johnny, I'd like to take you on holiday with me to the Kruger National Park on one condition...you are not allowed to look at the animals!'
'But that's what everybody does...we all go to the Game Reserve to see the wild animals!'
Lucy explained: 'why do we have to do what
everybody else does?
...we are going to look at and study the
insects...they've got insects there that you don't find
elsewhere...and I'll be taking my tree book with so we can identify the

indigenous trees and I will also bring along my bird book.'
Every night, Lucy would read some poetry aloud to Johnny.
It was so romantic, lying outside on the grass with Lucy pointing out the constellations and names of the stars.
This was a love affair too good to be true...yet, Johnny wasn't happy.
Lucy expected Johnny to give up the rock n roll music he loved and Johnny felt that he was losing his identity.
Although this new life with Lucy was very
exciting and interesting, Johnny

was not
prepared to give up the things he
so dearly loved and was
accustomed to for his
new-found love.
Now, do opposites attract?
Well, maybe they do but for Lucy
and Johnny, it just didn't work
out.

JUST FOR YOU

Darling

I dedicate my love to you

to make your life more beautiful

Your love means everything to
me

Your smile makes my world
brighter

Your kiss awakens my soul

Your touch is a very special magic

Baby, Take me in your arms

and let me love you!

Bring back the romantic

memories

As Time Goes By

Moonlight and love songs
Never out of date.
Hearts full of passion
Jealousy and hate.
Woman needs man
And man must have his mate
That no one can deny.
It's still the same old story

A fight for love and glory
A case of do or die.
The world will always welcome
lovers
As time goes by.

Music and words by Herman Hupfeld

PRECIOUS

*If you ever need
a helping hand in this world
If you ever need someone to
understand
I'm the one who loves you
I'm the one who cares
If you ever need a friend
Just know
I'll be there!*

The Twelfth Of Never

You ask how much I need you,
must I explain?
I need you, oh my darling, like
roses
need rain.
You ask how long I'll love you;
I'll tell you true:
Until the twelfth of never,
I'll still be loving you.
I'll love you till the bluebells
forget to bloom;

I'll love you till the clover has lost
its perfume.
I'll love you till the poets run out
of rhyme,
Until the twelfth of never
and that's a long, long time.

Jerry Livingston and Paul Francis Webster

Send a message
to your loved one

If only you knew how I care for
you
Then you might realize

that my love is true.

Darling, it feels so good to hold you

You will always be my friend

Meet me in your dreams tonight

I can't live without you

My happiness is you my love,

I could ask for nothing more.

Take me in your arms my darling

You're so beautiful

I love everything about you

Step right into my life

I'm so glad I found you

I have never been loved like this
before

I want my arms around you

Your love keeps lifting me higher
and higher

I'll make love to you,

whenever you want me to

I will always love you

I love to hear you call my name

Love will keep us together

I can't stop loving you

I'll do anything for you, because I love you

You are my endless love

I'm forever in love with you

You can have all of me

I want to make you feel my love

Love me tender

I love how you love me

Your love is precious

I love you madly

I want you, I need you, I love you

My love is without end

Only you can love me this way

You are the love of a lifetime

I can't get enough of your love

You are all I want

I love you just the way you are

You are always on my mind

I love you inside out

You're the one that I want

You are the sunshine of my life

I was made to love you

I need your love tonight

I've got a whole lot of love for you

You are in my heart

You are the one I give my heart to.

When our goal is to please each other, our love flourishes and grows.

You belong to my heart, now and forever

I can't live without your love

I think about you constantly

All I ever want is you

I'm missing you so very much

Roses are red
Violets are blue
Sugar is sweet
And so are you.

Let your love-life sizzle

with excitement and passion!

From the moment I saw you, I just knew

that you were my one in a million.

You complete my life in so many ways

and give me love that no one else could.

I am hopelessly in love with you.

I love you from head to toe

and more than you'll ever
know.

You are my heaven

Without you I am incomplete

 I want to live my life with you

Thanks for all you do

that makes my life happier

Hope your day
is just as awesome
as you are!

Tonight is all ours.
I can't wait to celebrate with
you.

You take my breath away,
Always.

I couldn't ask for a more
wonderful lover than you.

My heart is all yours.

Thanks for being you
and for being all mine.

I wish you were here for me
to make love to today.

I'm thinking of you lots!

I'm so grateful for you.

Thanks for sharing your life with me.

You're the best, and I'm so blessed to have you!

Do you know how often I think of you?
Always.

You're on my mind and in my heart.

I just wanted you to know that you're on my mind and in my prayers.

I'm thinking of you. And I'm just a text and a phone call away.

I'm here. And I've got some wine.

I'm here to help, if you need it.

I'm here for you no matter what!

Thanks for being you

I'm so grateful that God put you into my life

You make my world better every day

Everything I do is always better with you.

I love you to the moon and back.

I'm so thankful for you!

Thanks for being the person who inspires me so much.

You mean the world to me.

Clothes are overrated.
They always get in our way!

I am so glad to have you in my
life.

Sweetheart, I will always be
yours.

I would like to show you with my
body
how much I love you.

Thanks for loving me for who I
am.

My heart is yours today and
everyday.

I don't know what I would do
without you, but I know it
wouldn't be as fun.

You are a unique one-of-a-kind
gift
that cannot be matched.

My definition of love is you.

There's no one else in the world
who could make this day more
blessed,
than you!

Your arms are my paradise

Your voice is my comfort

Your strength is my safety.

Words cannot express how much you mean to me.

All you need is love. But a little chocolate now and then doesn't hurt.
Charles M. Schulz

On a scale of one to ten, I'd give you a nine — I'm the missing one that you need.

If I could rearrange the alphabet,
I would put U and I together.

Do you have a plaster? Because I scraped my knee

when I fell for you.

Sweetheart

You are my Lover,

Friend,

Guide,

Taxi-service,

Money-lender,

Dictionary,

Time-keeper,

Message-bureau

and no one

can ever take your place!

There is no one I like to lie in
bed with more, than you!

I think you are suffering from a
lack of
Vitamin ME.

My favorite place in all of the
world is in your arms.

You are the best partner
I could have ever asked for.

Suddenly all the love songs I
hear
are about you.

Nothing in my life has ever
meant as much to me as you
do.

I love it when you take me in
your arms and I know I'm
always safe there.

I will never forget the moment I
realized
that I love you.

You take my breath away.
Always.

For love, I'd do anything. For
you, I'd do more.

Come live in my heart, and pay
no rent.

I love you not only for what you
are but, for what I am when I'm
with you.

Unless you love someone,
nothing else makes sense.
E.E. Cummings

A VERY SPECIAL LOVE

Honey

I love you so very, very dearly.

Because of you...

My world has become more beautiful

My life is now more meaningful

I will never forget your kindness

Through all the sunsets of our lives

I will be adoring you

Without end.

'I LOVE YOU!'

You are the beginning of a life
long
romance.

We can't always choose our
teachers,
but if we could, I would choose
you all over again.

You are my first, my last, my
everything.

Included in this message is a

good amount of hugging,
kissing, and other fun things
we'll do later.

You are my love,

my dream,

my joy

and my desire.

I can't imagine living my life
without you.

About the Author

For more than 30 years, Bernard Levine has written the inspirational and romantic words published in greeting cards and posters, on sale both locally and internationally.

Bernard lives with his wife, Chrissie and cats, Whiskers, (Wikkie) Maggie Mae, Bo Peep, Benji and Stewart Little in sunny South Africa.

Bernard Levine is the author of 42 published books on sale both locally and internationally at more than 700 bookstores. Bernard's books have been translated into 12 languages and are also available as Audio-books.

Bernard Levine's Books

Awesome Love

Hidden Secrets of the Jewish World
Now Revealed

Passionately Praise Jesus

What would you do for the one
you love?

Who took the name of God out of
the Bible?

100's of Opportunities for you to
make money

How to witness to Jews about
Jesus...
what Christians need to know

You are not supposed to know
the Secrets of the Jews (Secrets
of the Jewish World) (Volume 3)
Intimate Sex Secrets of the Jews

The Best of Bernard Levine

The Secrets of the Jews: (What Christians don't know about the Jewish religion, traditions and way of life)

How to find a job quickly and easily

Make money collecting books, get free celebrity autographs and more!

Expert Telemarketing: How to Urgently Get Lots of Sales Appointments

The Secrets of the Jewish World (What Christians don't know about the Jewish religion, traditions and way of life Book 1)

Why I left the Jewish religion to follow Jesus

How to meet your soul mate: There is someone very special waiting to meet you

There Is Nothing to Pay!: Get It All for Free...

Meet Freddy the friendly Fireman

How to please your loved one (in 100 different ways): The magic of romantic love

Children love Nursery Rhymes

Children love to tell jokes

Get paid for the poems you write

How To Receive Your Miracle

The Fun Conversation Book

Change Your Destiny

A Book Full of Wonderful Exciting
Surprises

Meet Tommy the funny Toy
Maker

How to get paid appearing in TV
Ads
and Soapies

The Secrets of Life: Inspiration
you will never forget!

FUN By The TON!

Make money collecting
everyday easy to find items
The World's Best Loved
Inspiration

Save the Jews: What Jewish
people do not know about Jesus

Do you remember?: All the fun
stuff is here!

Children Love to Sing: Teach your
children the songs you sang
when you were a child

How to make your life more exciting

You can never say 'Thank You' enough to Jesus

The Jewish Confidential Files never published before!

When you pray, God sends angels

Did you live? Did you love? Did it matter?

Darling, I want you to know how very special you are to me

Dedication

To my darling wife, Chrissie

Thank you for all your love and kindness

To our precious cats,

Whiskers(Wikkie),

Maggie Mae,Bo Peep,Benji and

Stewart Little

You give us so much joy.

I love you all so dearly.

Sincerely from the heart

Bernard